COUNTING

Follow That Fish!

Based on the Math Monsters™ public television series, developed in cooperation with the National Council of Teachers of Mathematics (NCTM).

by John Burstein

Reading consultant: Susan Nations, M.Ed., author/literacy coach/consultant

Math curriculum consultants: Marti Wolfe, M.Ed., teacher/presenter; Kristi Hardi-Gilson, B.A., teacher/presenter

WEEKLY WR READER®
EARLY LEARNING LIBRARY

Please visit our web site at: **www.earlyliteracy.cc**
**For a free color catalog describing Weekly Reader® Early Learning Library's list
of high-quality books, call 1-877-445-5824 (USA) or 1-800-387-3178 (Canada).**
Weekly Reader® Early Learning Library's fax: (414) 336-0164.

Library of Congress Cataloging-in-Publication Data

Burstein, John.
    Counting: follow that fish! / by John Burstein.
       p. cm. — (Math monsters)
    Summary: The four math monsters show how to count as they help Cal figure out
the number of pets in his pet shop.
      ISBN 0-8368-3806-8 (lib. bdg.)
      ISBN 0-8368-3821-1 (softcover)
      1. Counting—Juvenile literature. [1. Counting.] I. Title.
QA113.B887   2003
513.2'11—dc21
                                                  2003045012

This edition first published in 2004 by
Weekly Reader® Early Learning Library
330 West Olive Street, Suite 100
Milwaukee, WI 53212 USA

Text and artwork copyright © 2004 by Slim Goodbody Corp. (www.slimgoodbody.com).
This edition copyright © 2004 by Weekly Reader® Early Learning Library.

Original Math Monsters™ animation: Destiny Images
Art direction, cover design, and page layout: Tammy Gruenewald
Editor: JoAnn Early Macken

Printed in the United States of America

1 2 3 4 5 6 7 8 9 07 06 05 04 03

You can enrich children's mathematical experience by working with
them as they tackle the Corner Questions in this book. Create
a special notebook for recording their mathematical ideas.

Counting and Math
Young children count by pointing, touching, and grouping objects.
In this story, the monsters model a variety of these
counting strategies.

Meet the Math Monsters™

ADDISON

Addison thinks
math is fun.
"I solve problems
one by one."

Mina flies
from here to there.
"I look for answers
everywhere."

MINA

MULTIPLEX

Multiplex
sure loves to laugh.
"Both my heads
have fun with math."

Split is friendly
as can be.
"If you need help,
then count on me."

SPLIT

We're glad you want to take a look
at the story in our book.

We know that as you read, you'll see
just how helpful math can be.

Let's get started. Jump right in!
Turn the page, and let's begin!

The Math Monsters loved to go to the pet store.
They always found something new to see. One
sunny day, they went for a visit.

As they walked along, they sang,
"Going to the pet store
is fun as fun can be.
We will open up the door
and see what we can see:
guppies, puppies,
pretty kitties,
parakeets that tweet.
Going to the pet store
is such a special treat."

Do you have a pet? What kinds of pets do you like?

The Math Monsters walked inside. They saw their Uncle Cal Q. Later, the owner of the store.

"Hello, Math Monsters," he said. "Today I am counting all the fish in my store."

"Can we help?" asked Addison.
"We love to count."
　"Sure," said Uncle Cal.

How will
the monsters
count the fish?

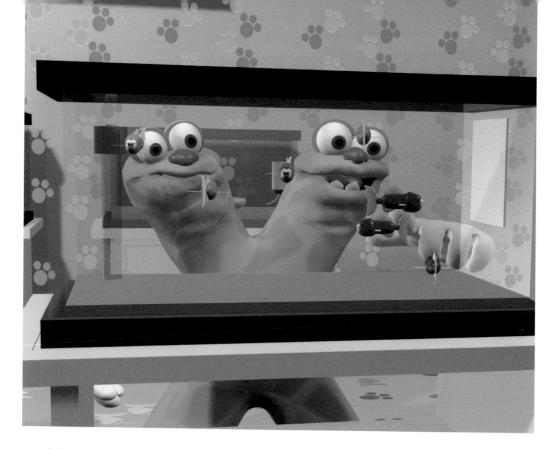

Multiplex went to the first tank.

"I will count these fish," he said.

"I will write the number down," said Mina.

Multiplex began to count. "1, 2, 3, 4, 5, 6, 7, 8, 9, 10, 11, 12, 13, 14."

"Fourteen? Are you sure?" asked Mina.

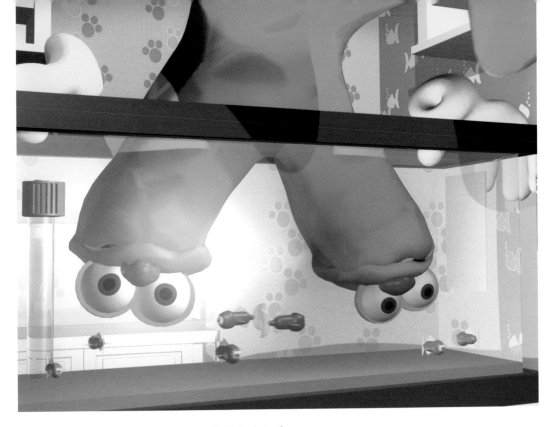

"I will count again," Multiplex said. "1, 2, 3, 4, 5, 6, 7, 8, 9, 10."

"The first time, you counted fourteen fish. Now you counted ten," said Mina.

"I know," said Multiplex. "It is hard to count moving fish."

Why is Multiplex having trouble counting the swimming fish?

"The fish swim around and around,
back
and forth,
this way
and that.
I cannot keep track of them," said Multiplex.

"There must be something we can do," said Mina.

Can you think of a way to help the monsters?

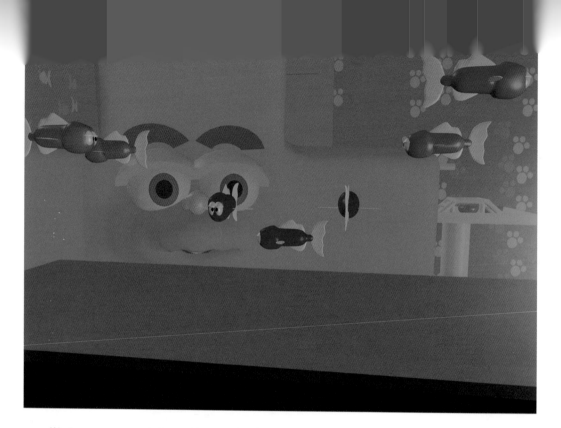

"I have an idea," said Addison. "We can use the colors of the fish to help us keep track as we count."

"What do you mean?" asked Split.

"Even as the fish swim, it is easy to see that there are only two red fish, three blue fish, and two green fish," he said.

"How many does that add up to?" asked Split.

"I think it will help if I draw a picture," said Mina. "I will draw the two red fish, the three blue fish, and the two green fish."

"Now it is much easier to count them all," said Split.

How many fish are in the tank? How does the picture help?

13

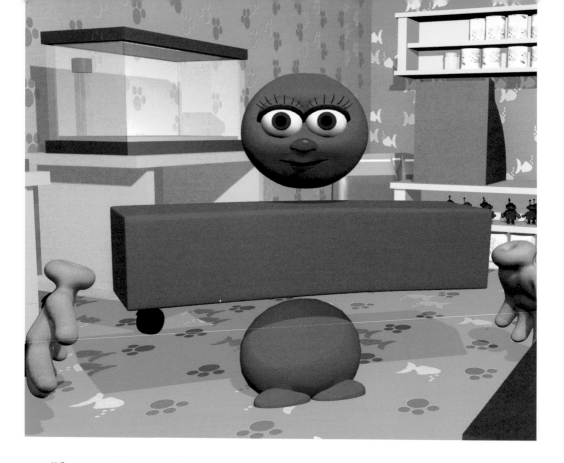

"Seven," said Split. "There are seven fish in all."
"Let's count the fish in the next tank," said Addison.

"I think this tank has more fish," said Addison.

"I do not want to draw any more pictures of fish," said Mina.

"Can we keep track in another way?" asked Split.

How can the monsters keep track of the fish without drawing a picture of each one?

"We can use tally marks that match the color of the fish," said Addison.

He looked at the tank. He said, "I see five red fish."

Mina made five red tally marks.

"I see three blue fish," said
Multiplex.

Mina made three blue tally marks.

"I see two green fish," said Split.

Mina made two green tally marks.

How many fish are in the tank?

"Ten fish in that tank," said Split.

"Oh, no!" Multiplex said. "The fish in this tank are all the same color."

"They are jumping fish," said Uncle Cal. "Each time you blow a whistle, one fish will jump out of the tank and into the tank next to it."

He gave each monster a whistle.

How can the monsters use the whistles to help them count?

19

"Each time you whistle and a fish jumps, you can count it," said Uncle Cal.

Split blew her whistle — toot! A fish jumped.

"One fish, one mark," said Mina.

"Let's all blow our whistles at once. Then four fish will jump," said Addison.

They all blew their whistles.

If Mina adds four more tally marks, how many will there be?

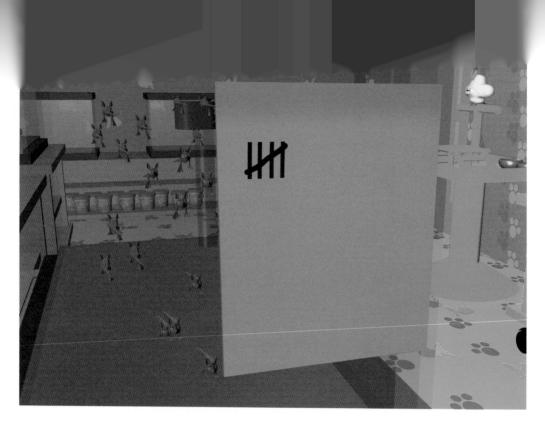

"Five fish so far," said Mina.

The monsters kept counting. They counted twenty fish in the tank.

Then they counted all the fish in the store. When they were done, they told Uncle Cal how many they had counted.

"Thank you very much," said Uncle Cal.
"Come back and see me soon."

The monsters walked home. They sang
about the things they liked to count.

"Trees we see, friends we meet,
signs and lines across the street,
the kinds of foods we like to eat,
shoes we see on people's feet.
We can count. So can you.
Counting things is fun to do."

What kinds of things do you like to count?

ACTIVITIES

Page 5 Reflecting on familiar settings helps children connect to a story. Ask about children's visits to pet stores. Have them draw or list the kinds of pets they have seen.

Page 7 Discuss why stores take inventory. At home, count cups, shoes, or spoons. At school, count pencils, pens, or paper clips. What else might the monsters count?

Page 9 Books present still images. To help children understand the difficulty of counting moving objects, show them a real-life situation, such as ducks on a pond, birds in flight, or children on a playground.

Pages 11, 13 Provide construction paper and scissors for children to cut out two red, three blue, and two green squares. Ask them to sort by colors. Show how this can make counting easier.

Page 15 Children may not use the same strategies as the monsters. Help them see how their own creative solutions have merit and value.

Page 17 Make colored paper squares. Have children make colored tally marks to match the squares. Practice counting tally marks. Explain that when the tally reaches five, the last mark ties the bundle together.

Pages 19, 21 Remind children that there are many ways to count groups of objects (one at a time or in small groups) and many ways to show what has been counted (pictures, tally marks, or numerals).

Page 23 Encourage children to apply Math Monster strategies to their own counting and number representation.